Do The DOodles

Not Your Ordinary
Coloring Book

by

Peggy Campbell

DEDICATION

For
Amy Lea Campbell
Loved and Missed

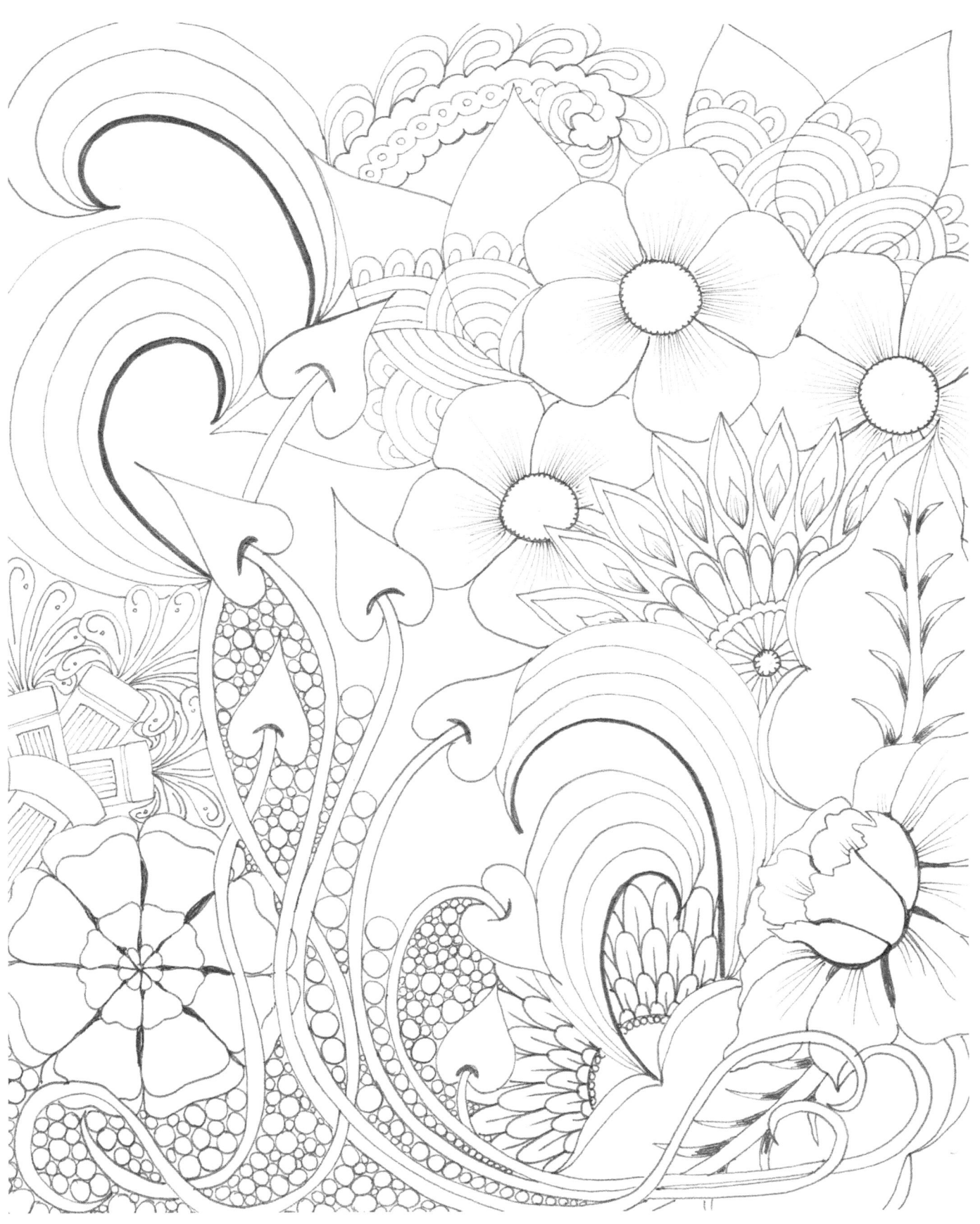

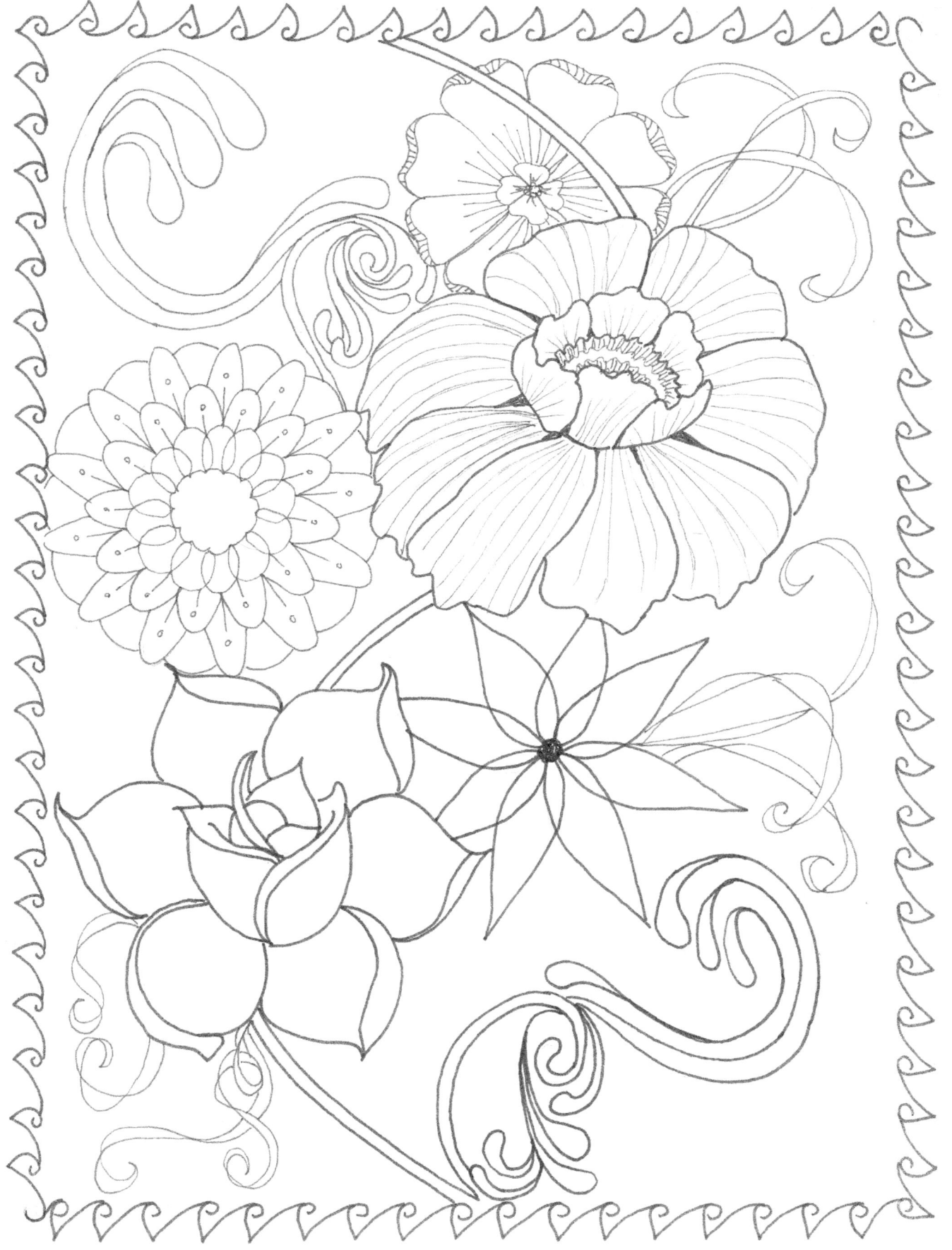

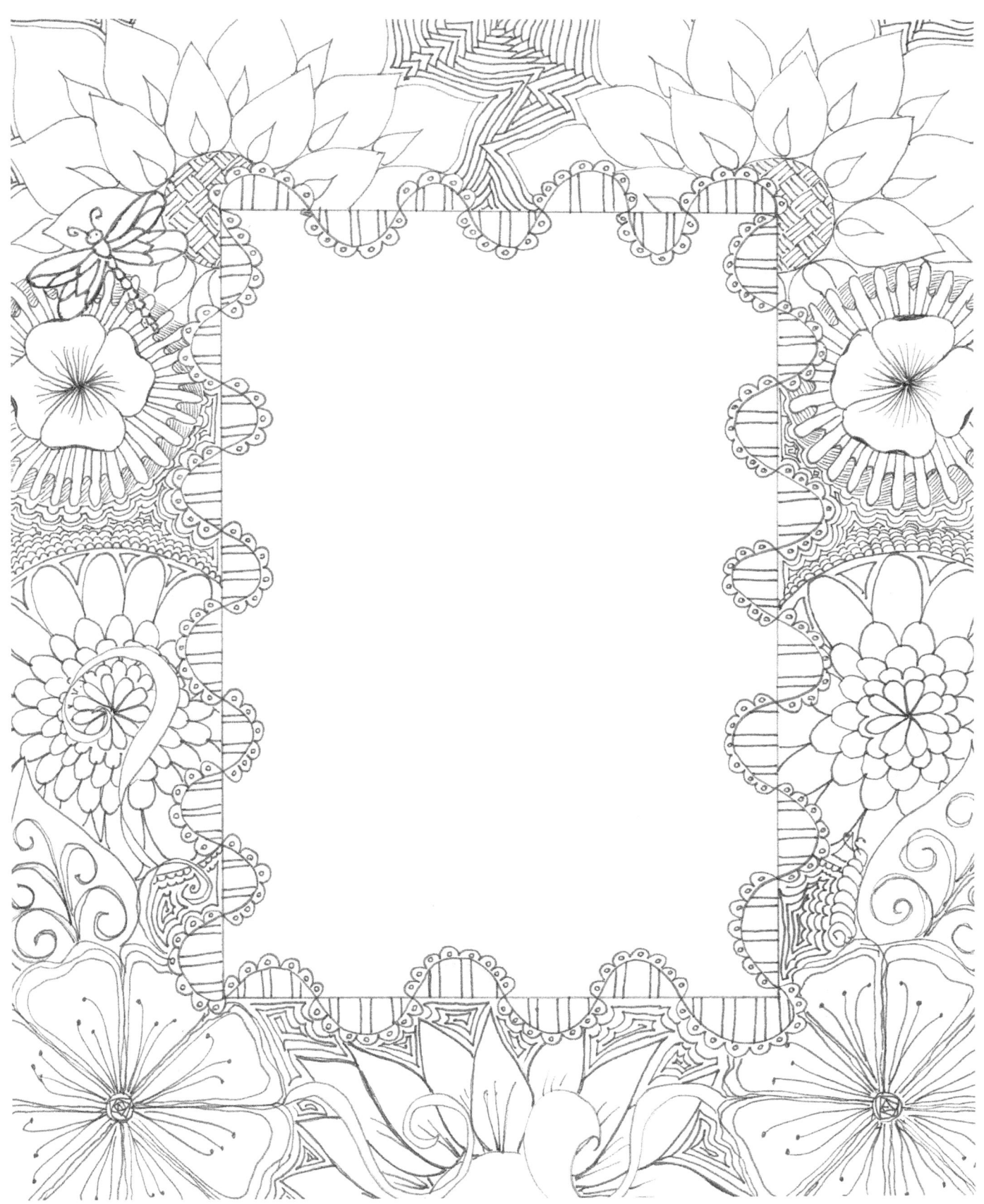

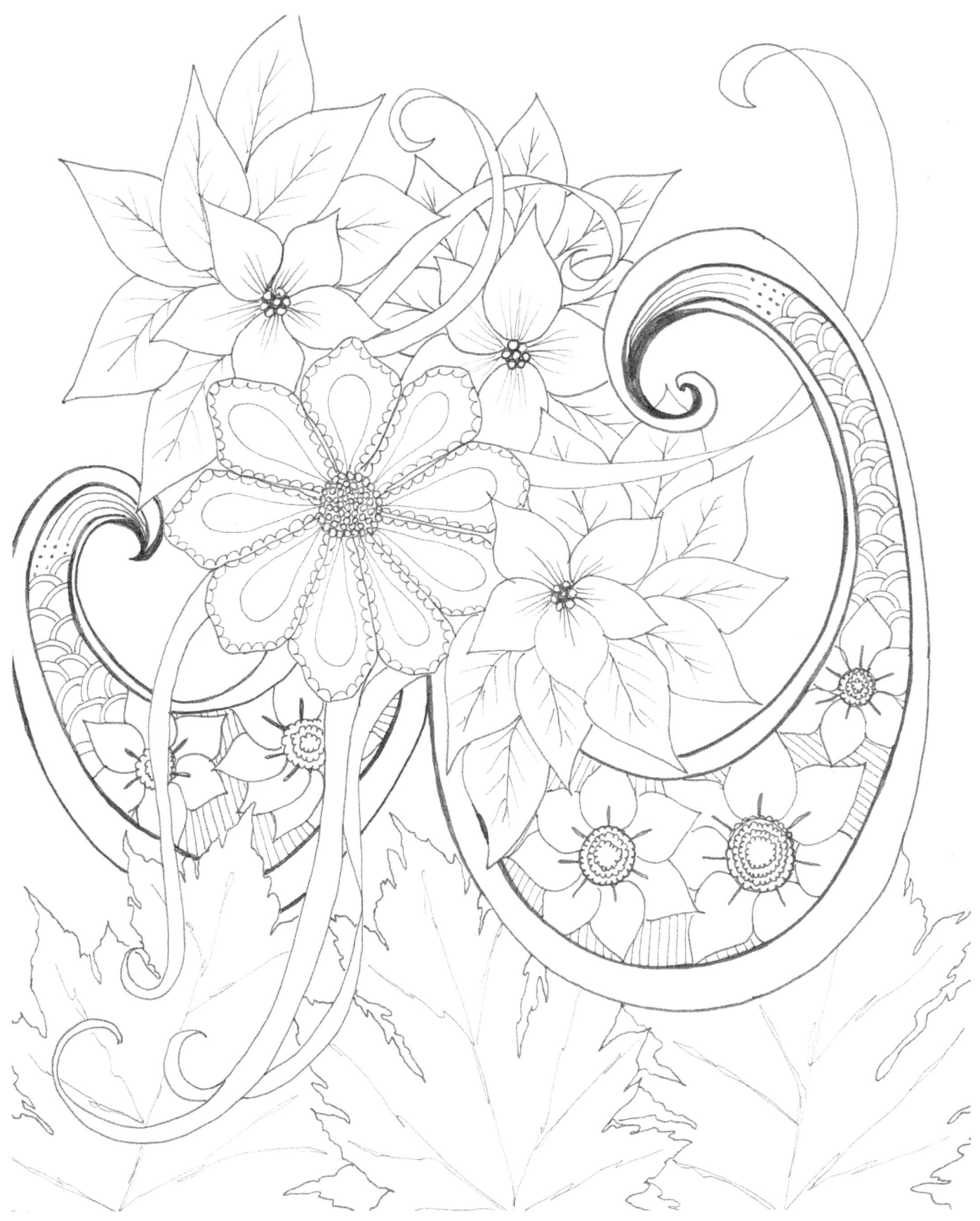

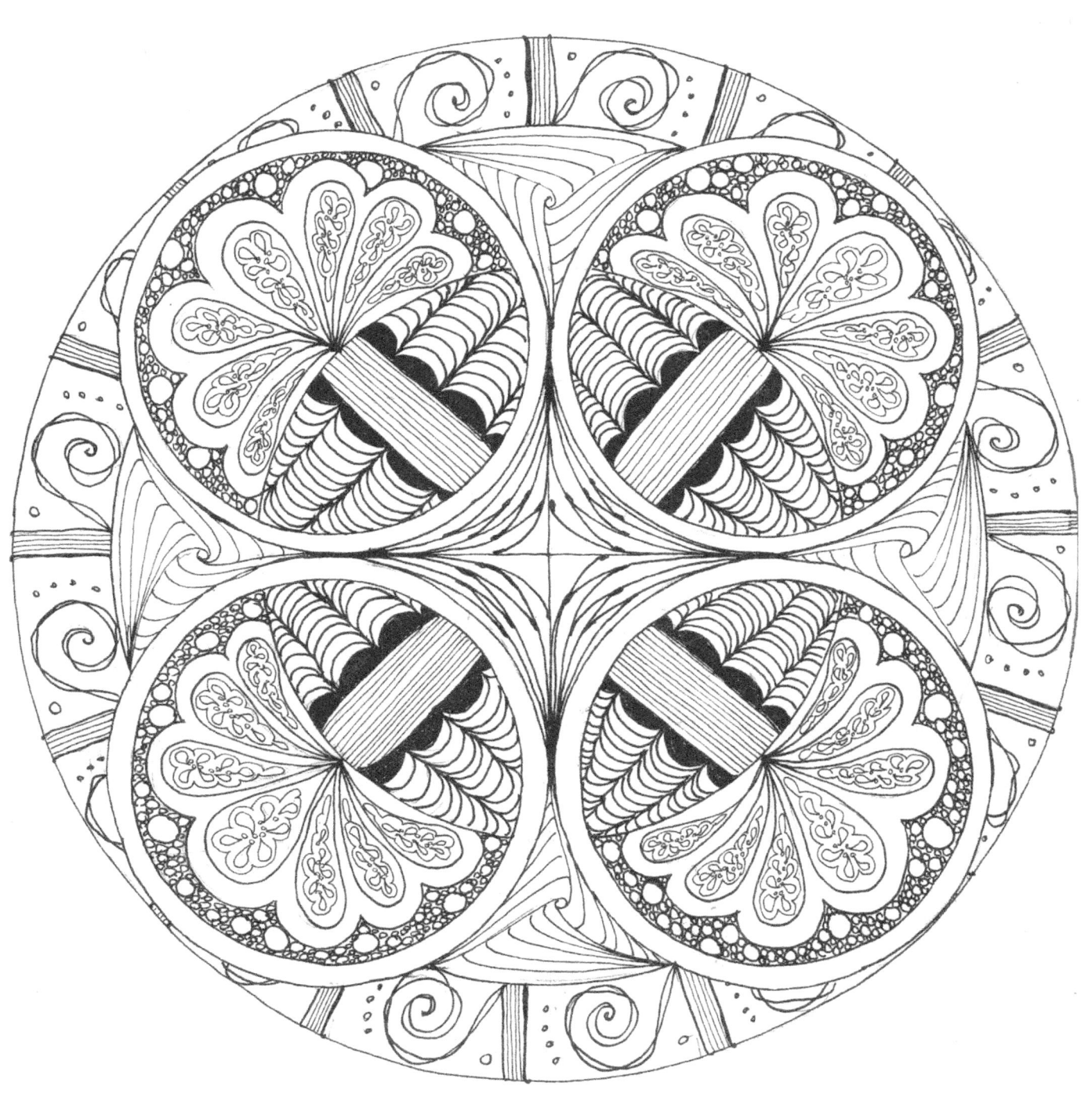

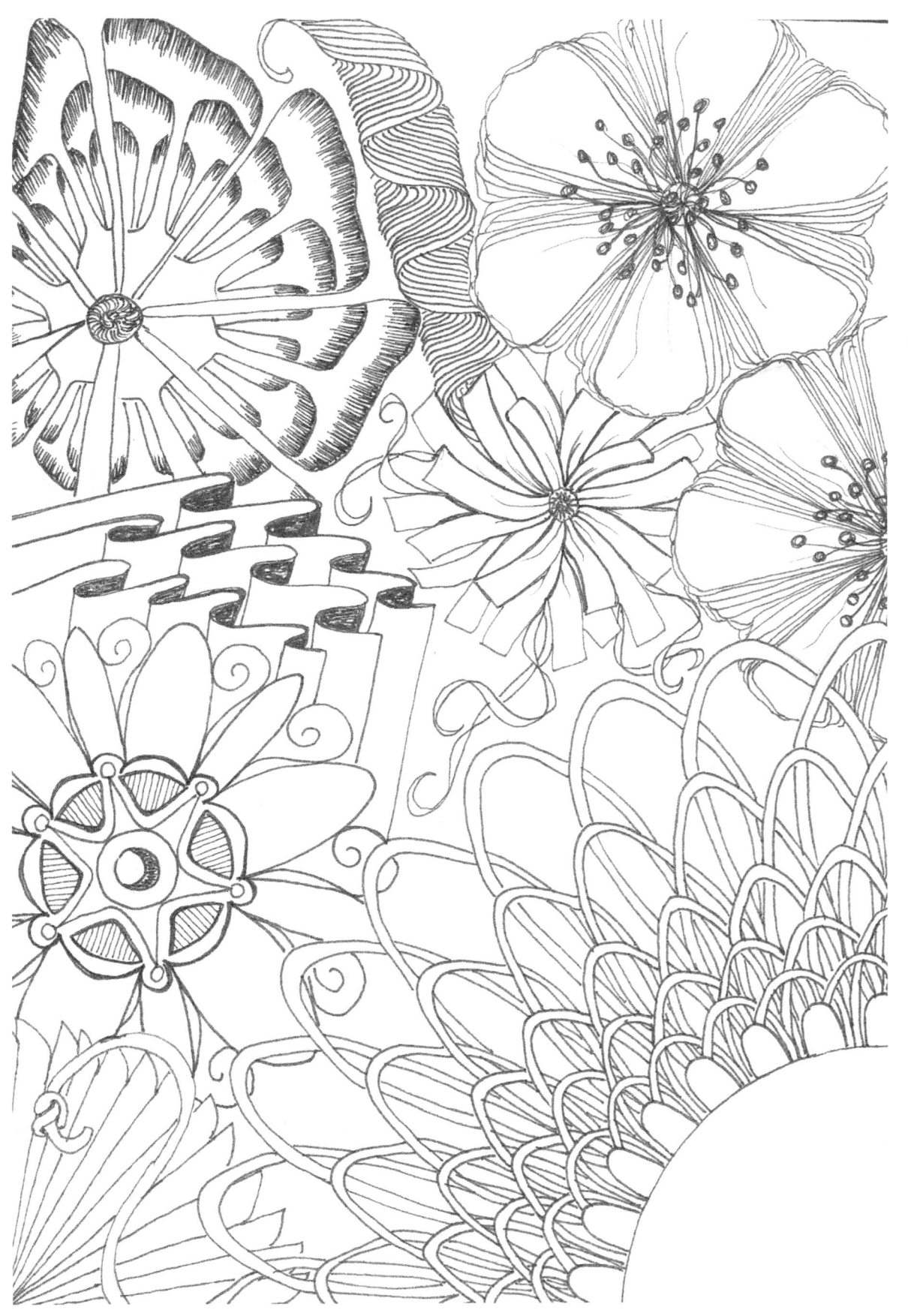

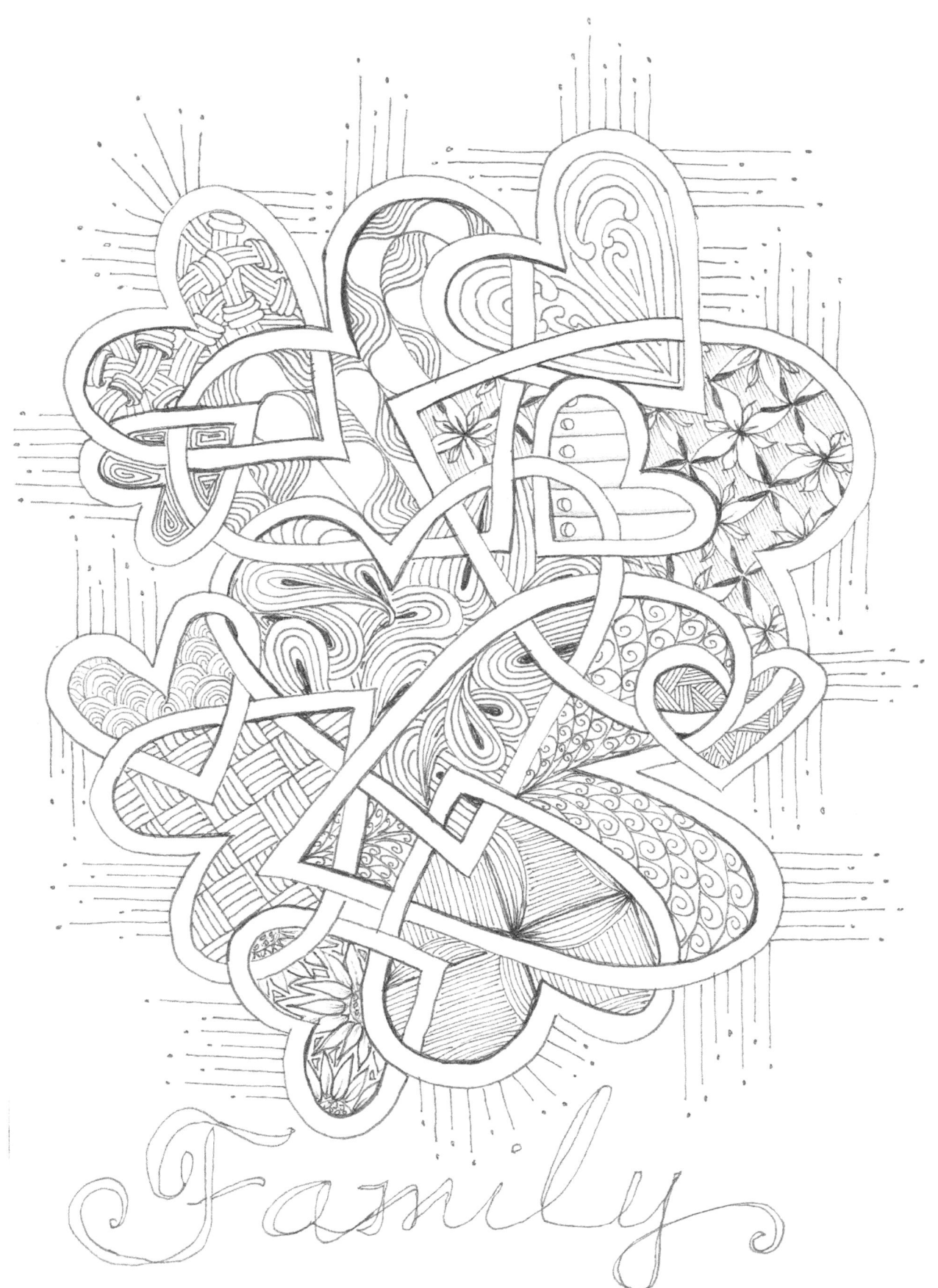

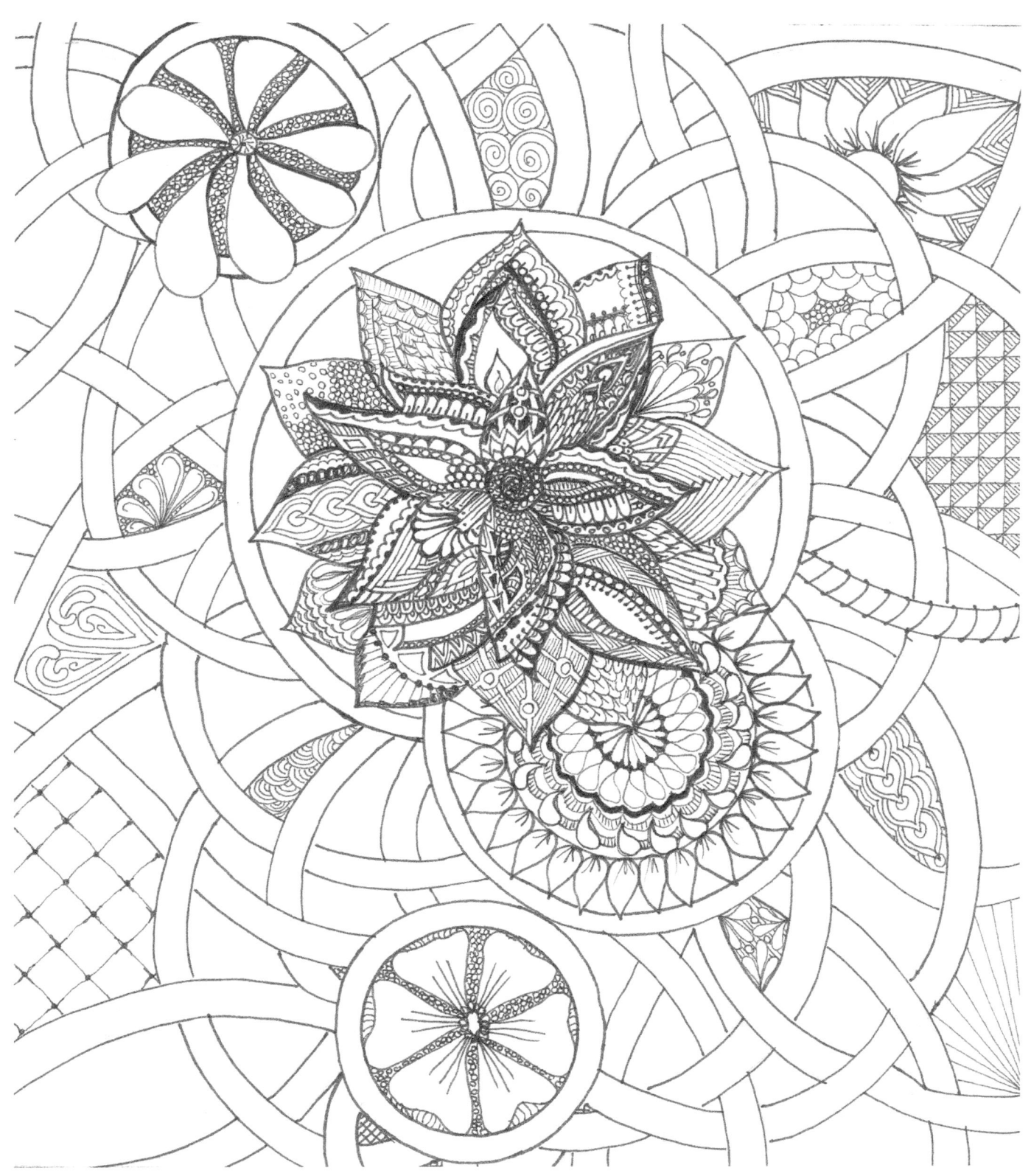

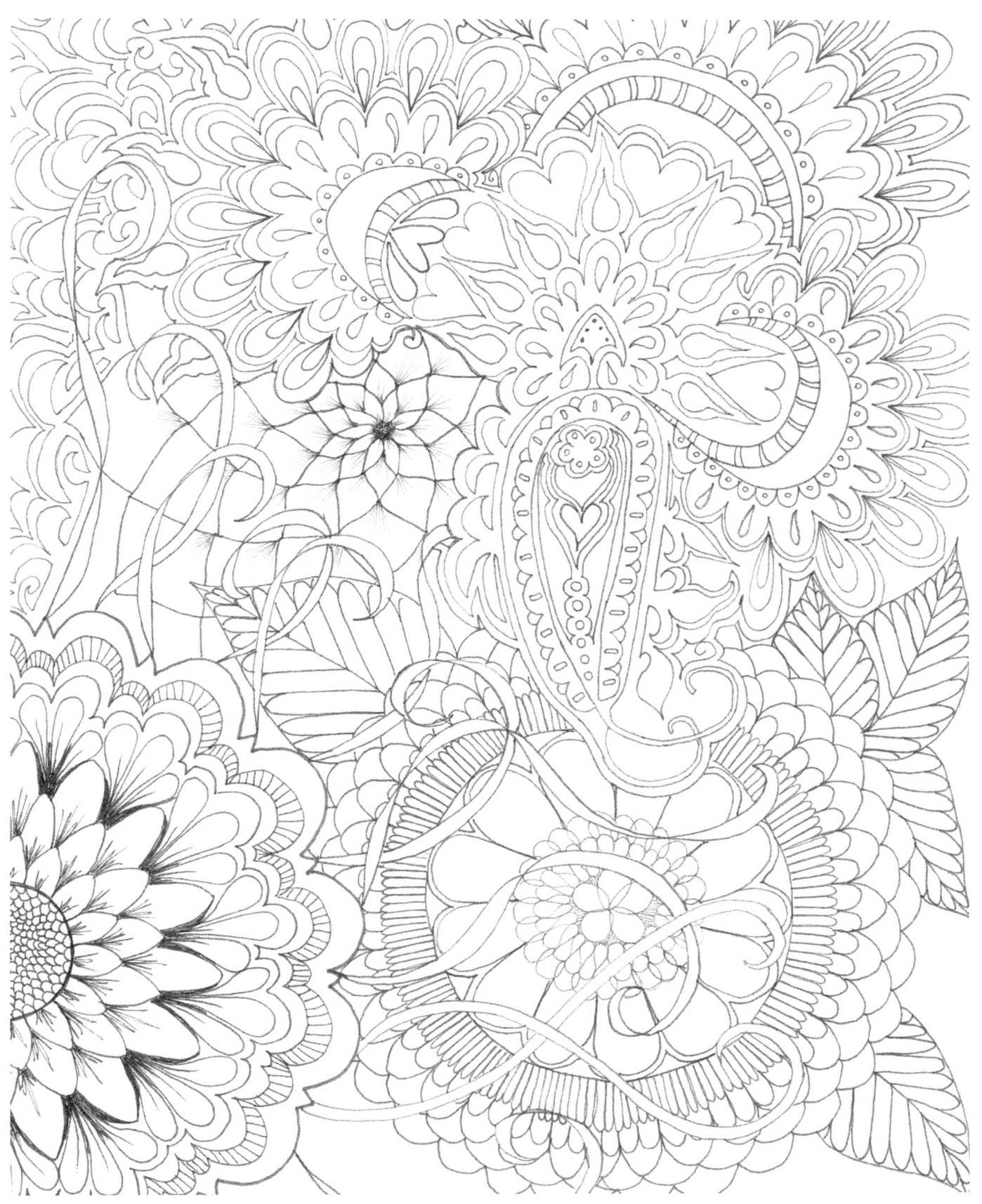

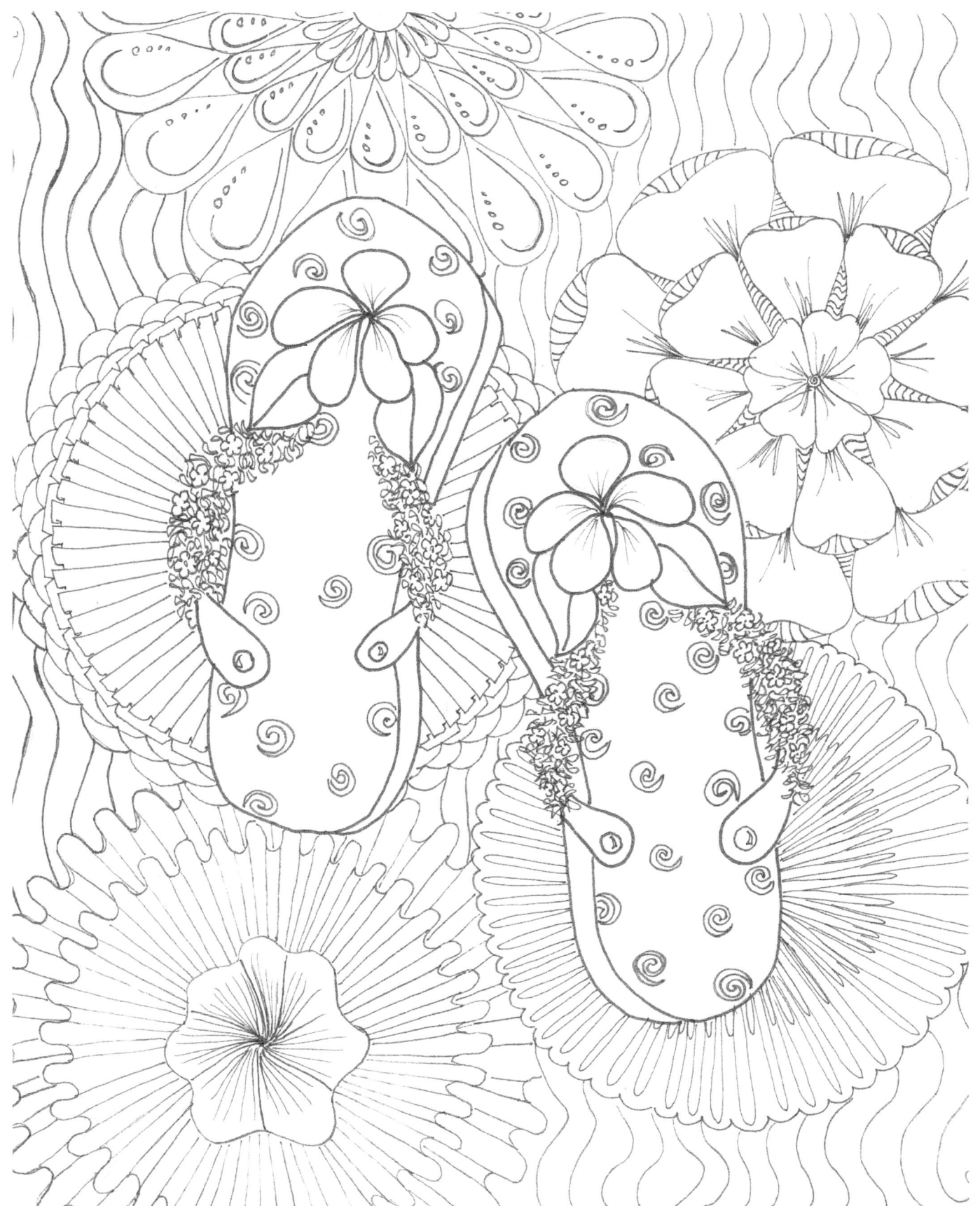

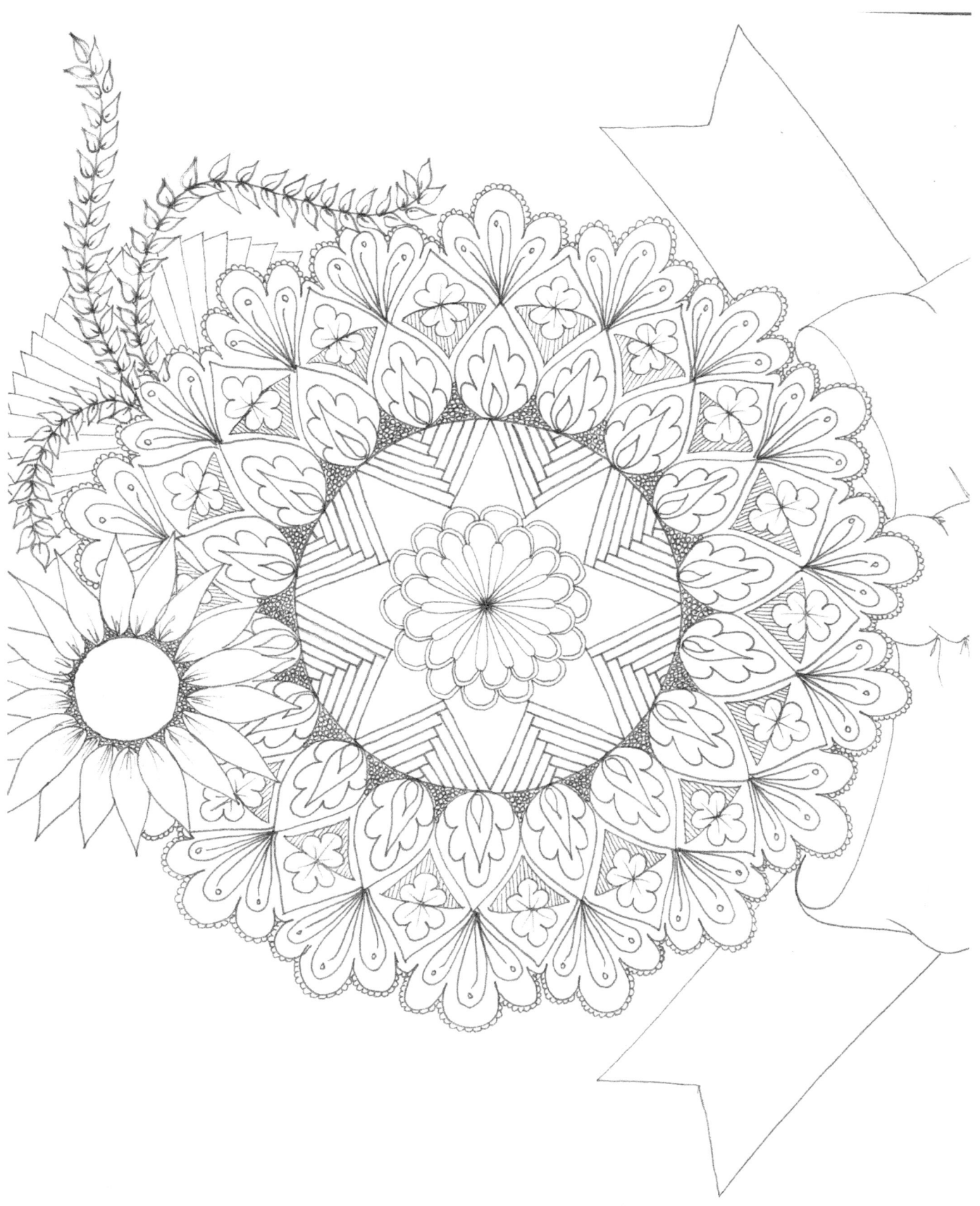

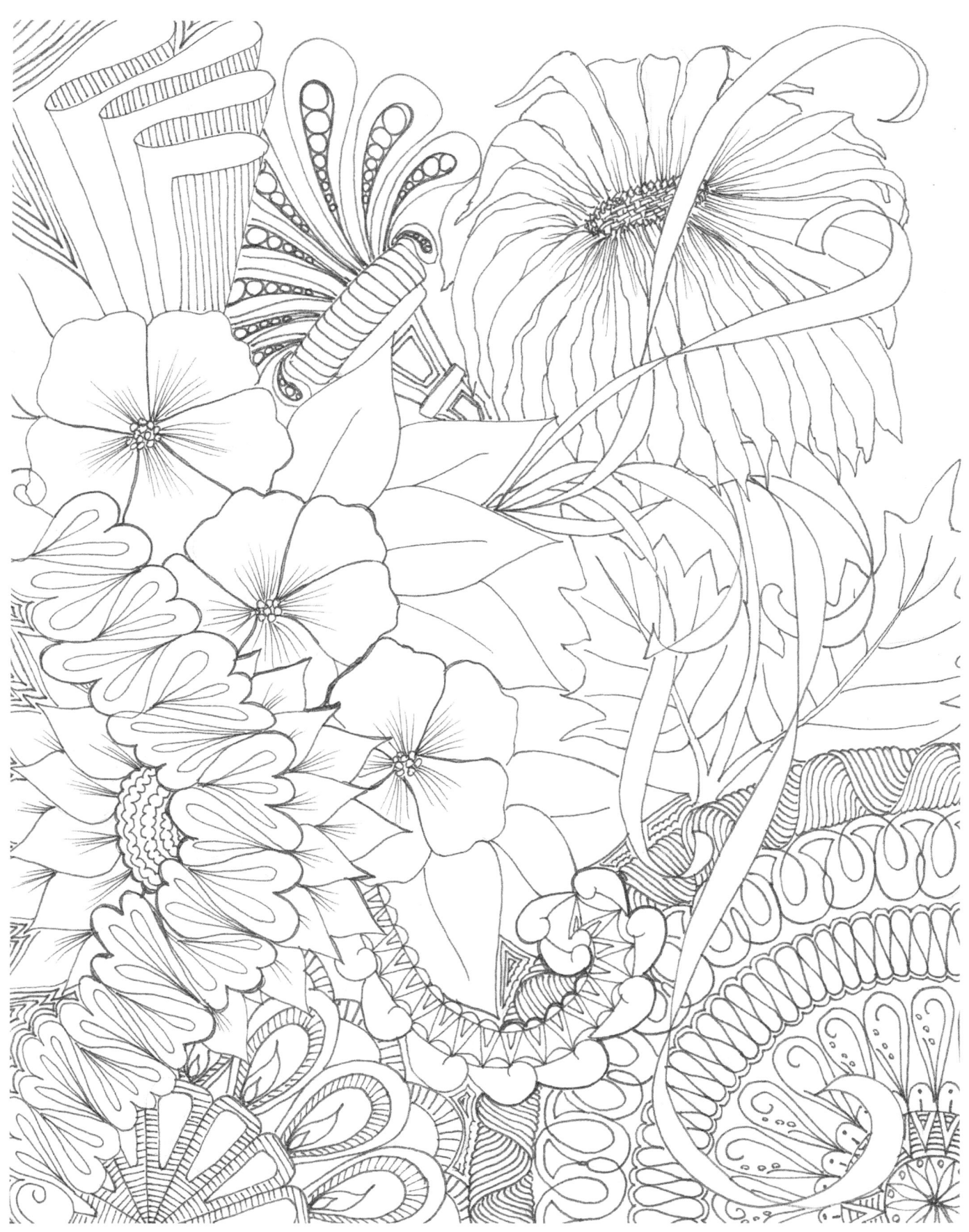

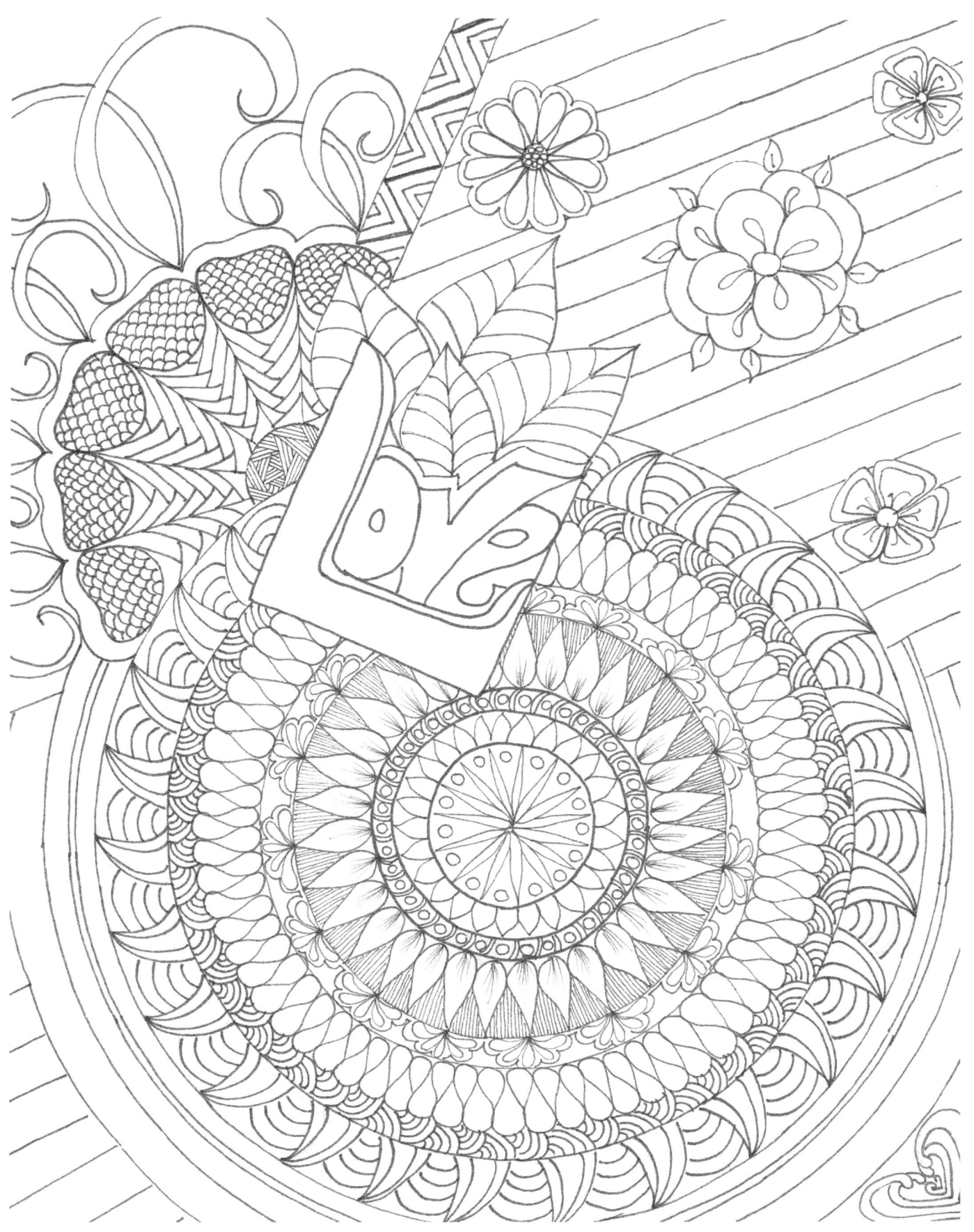

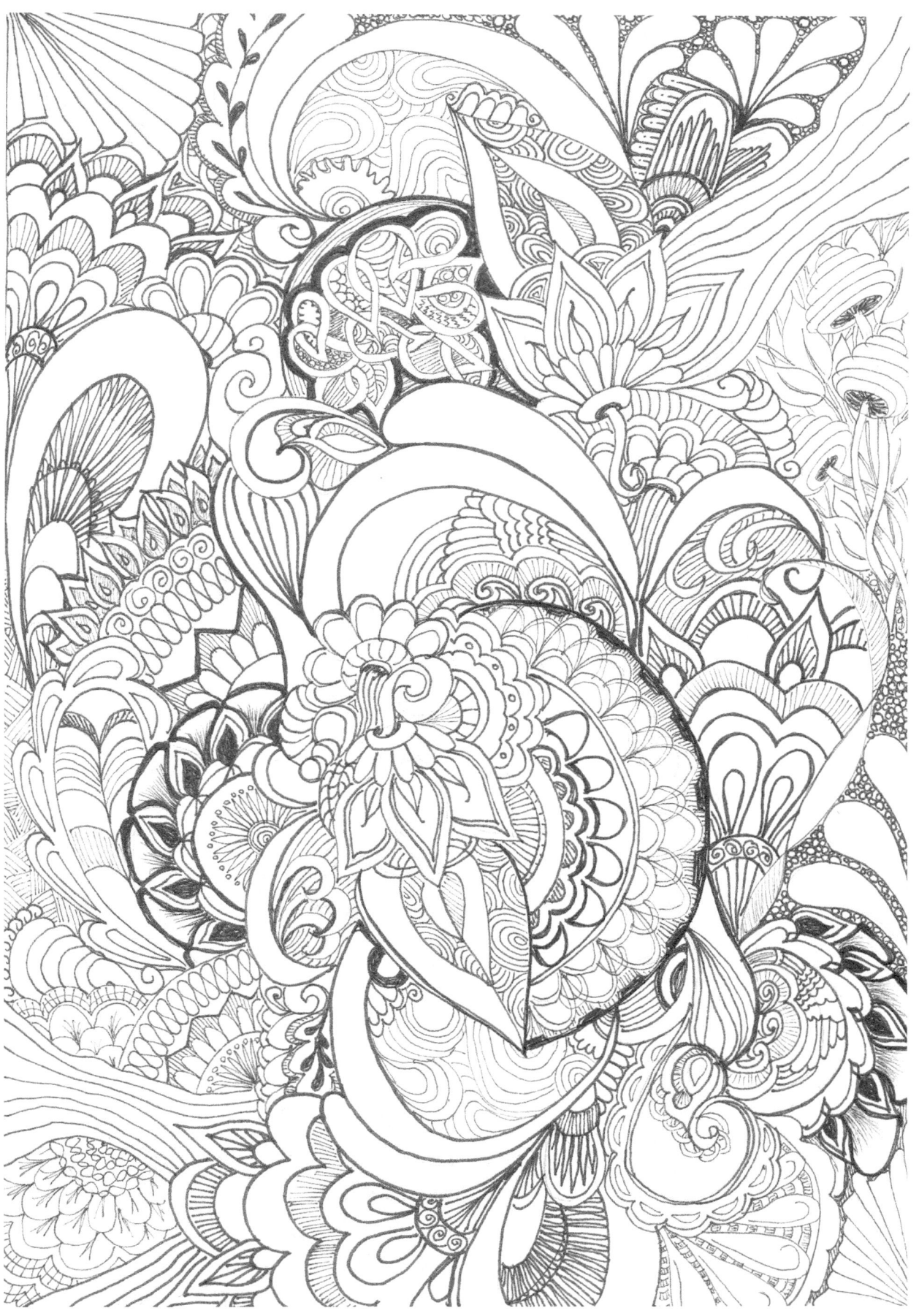

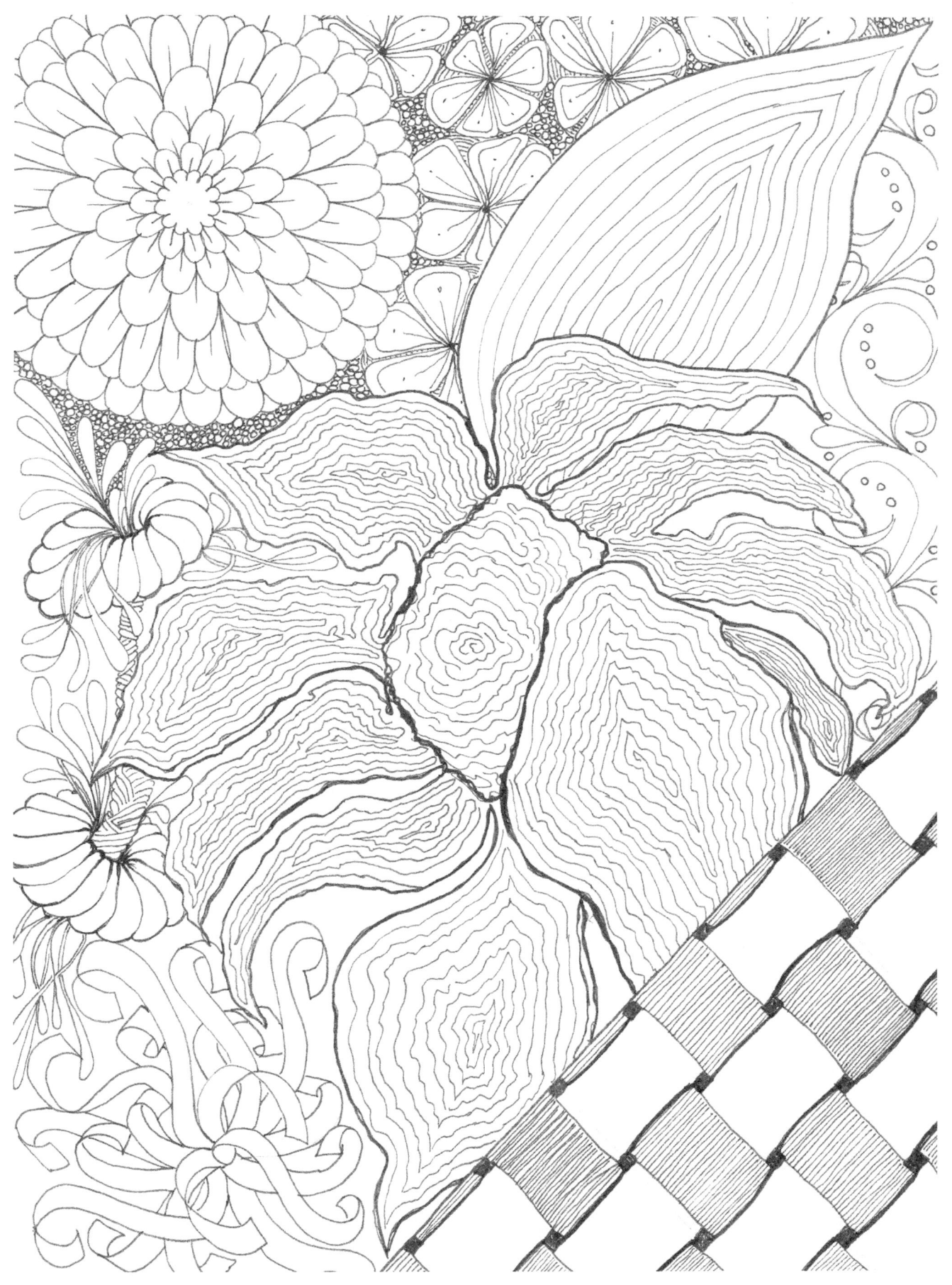

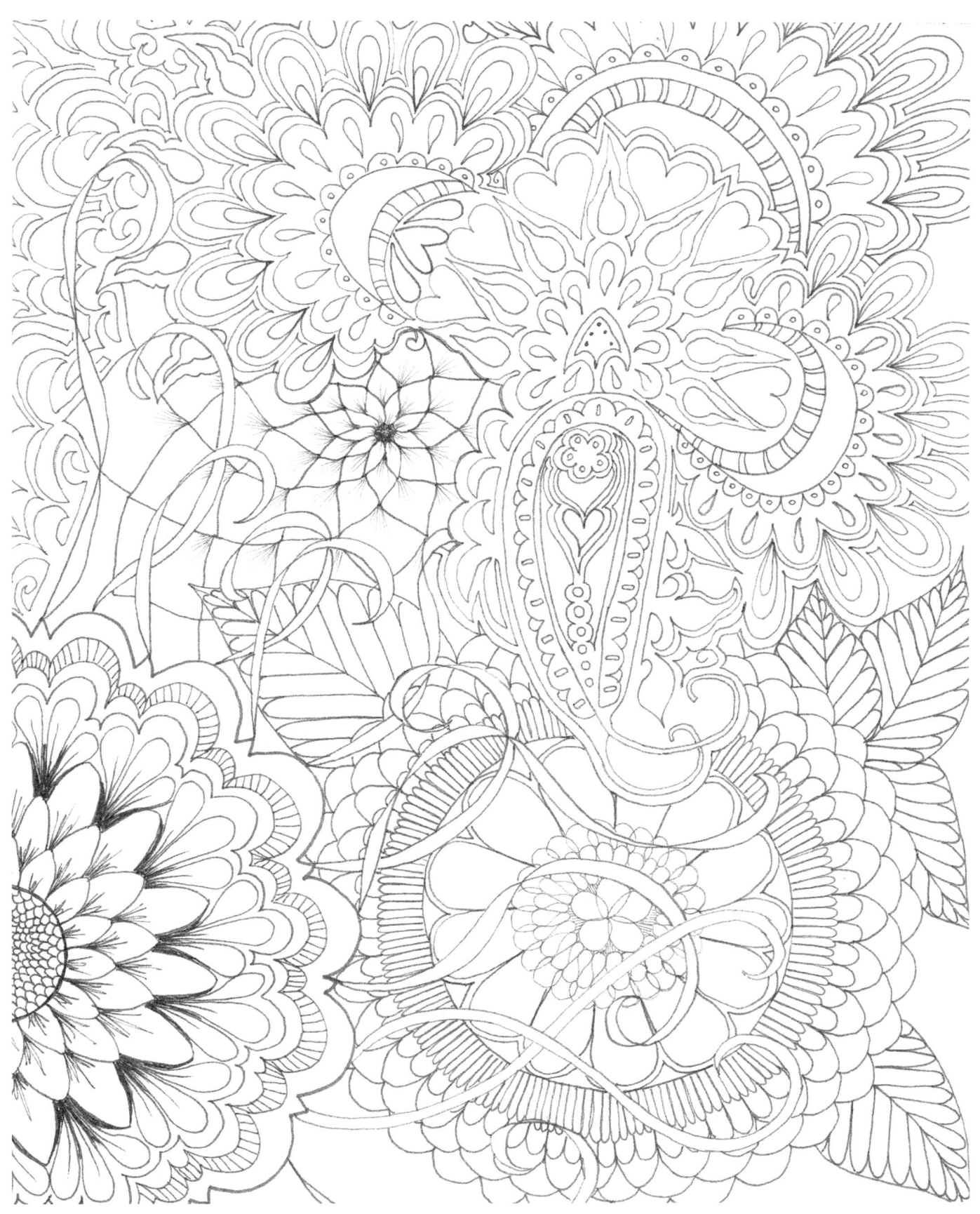

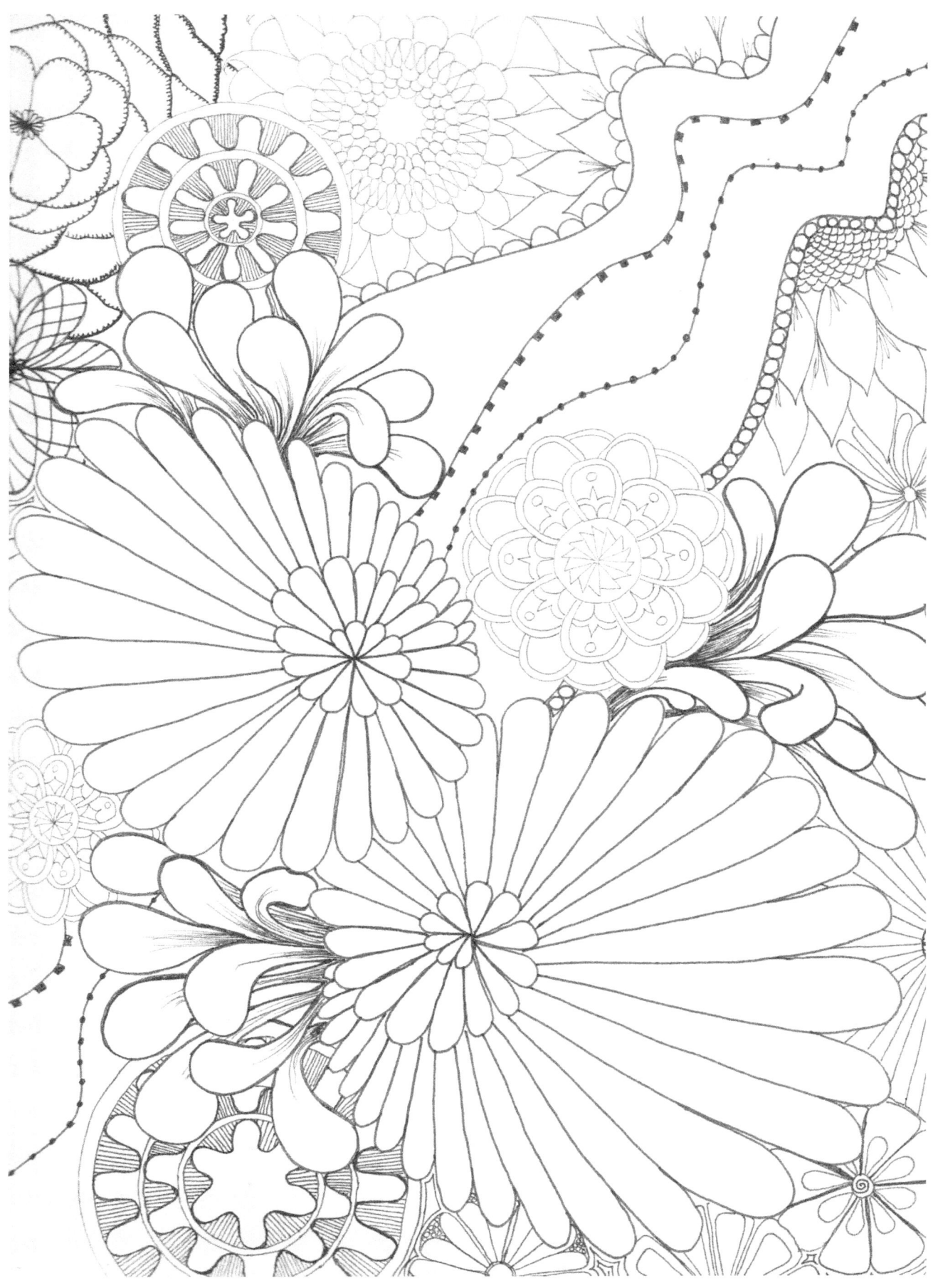

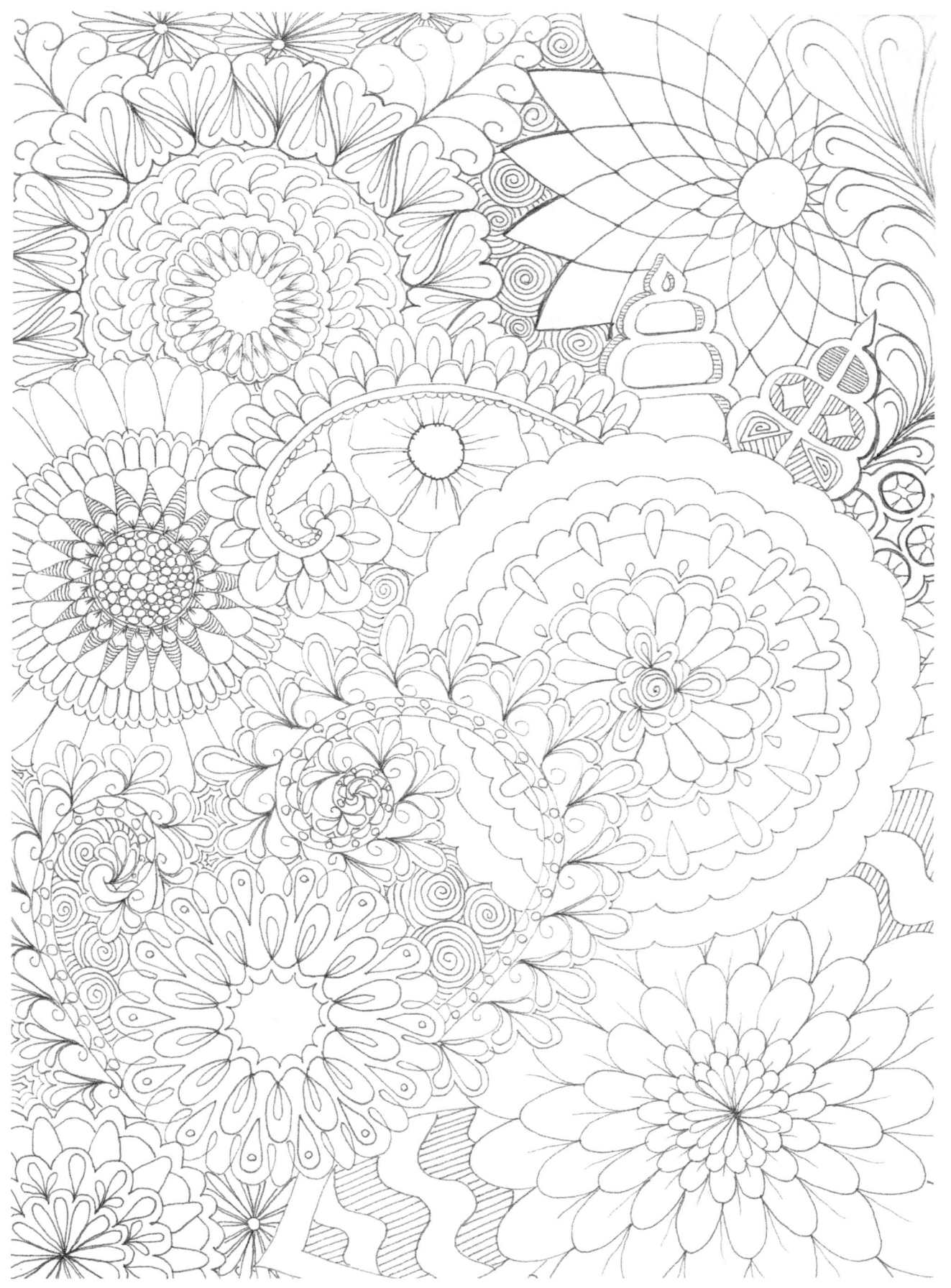

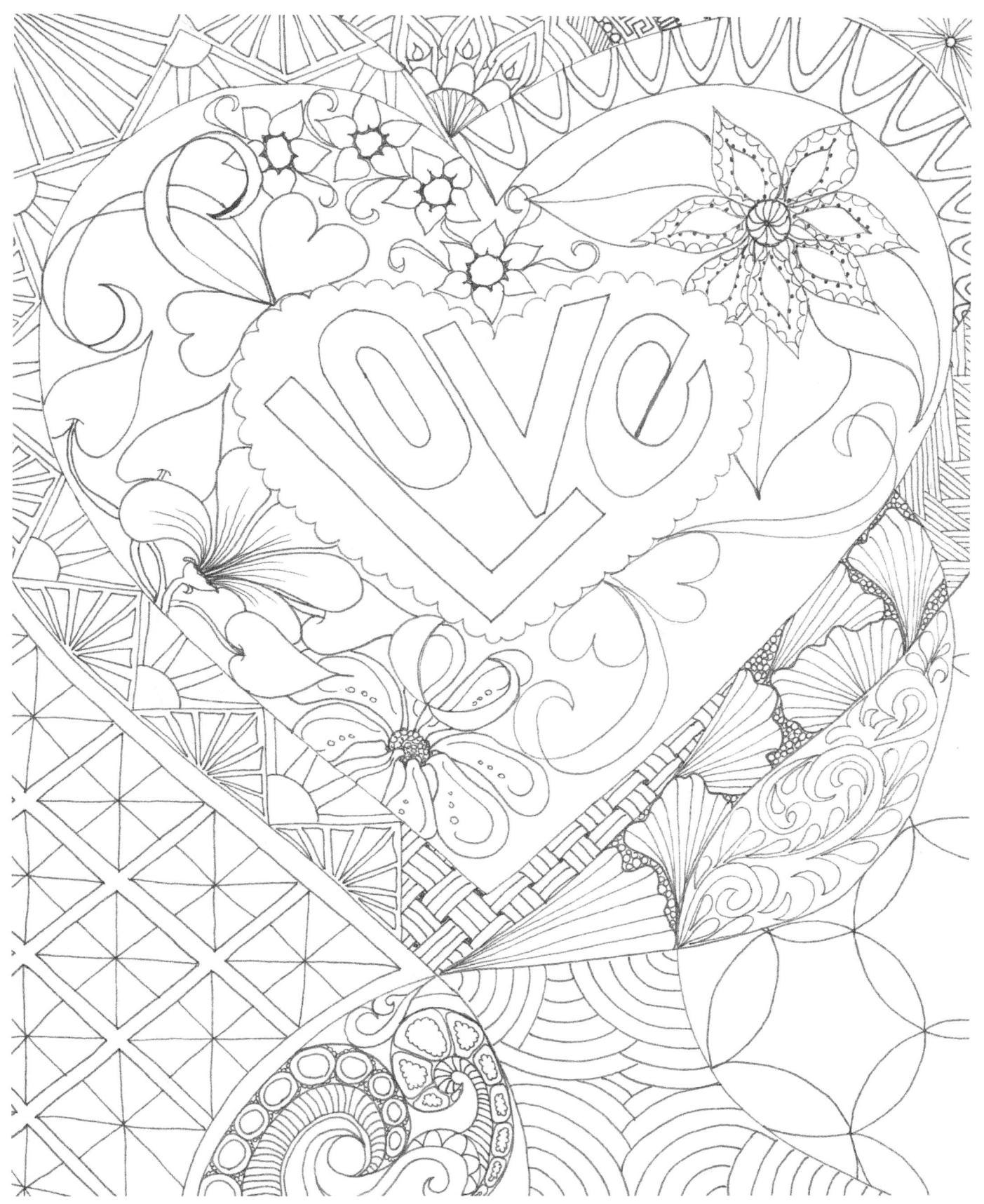

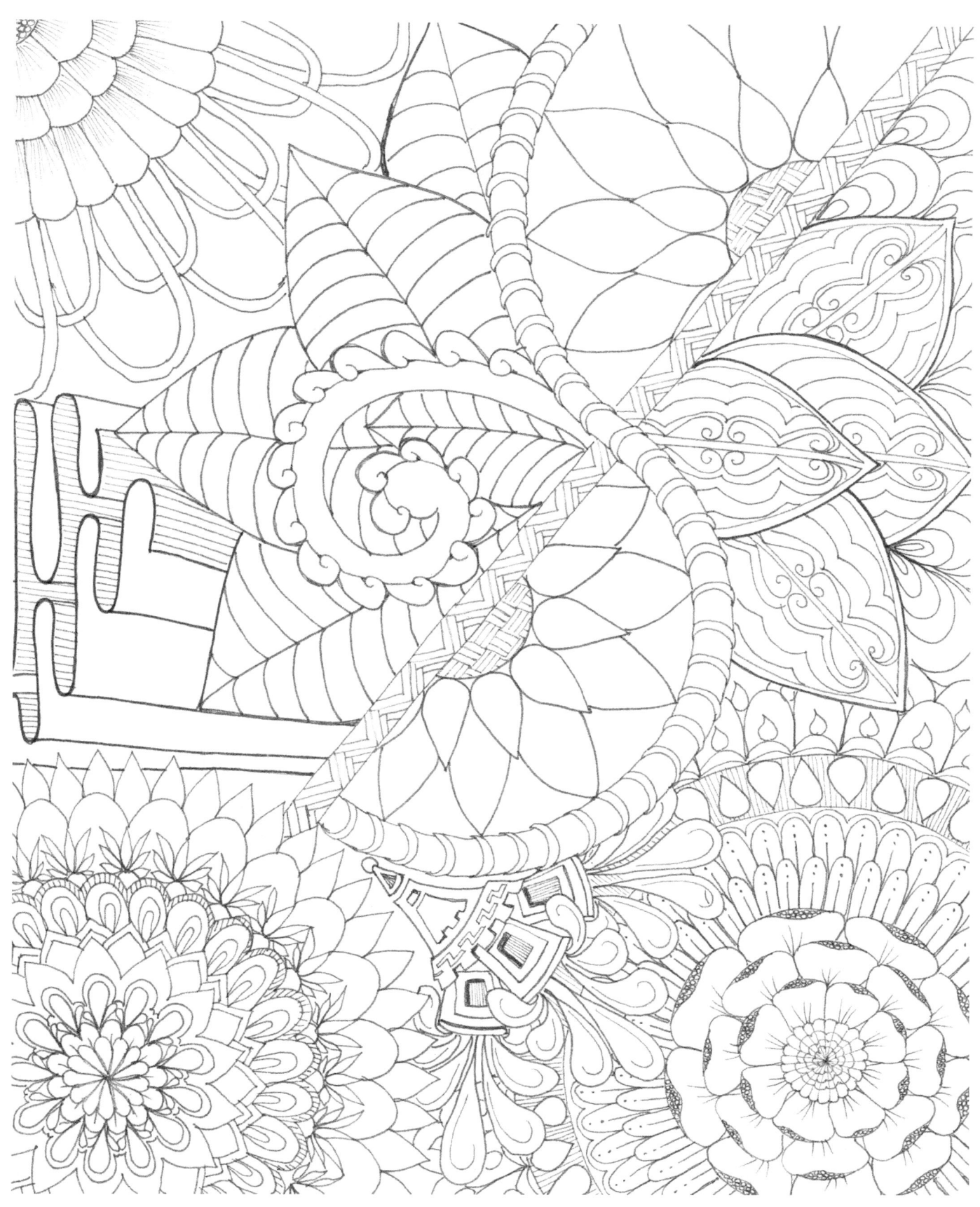

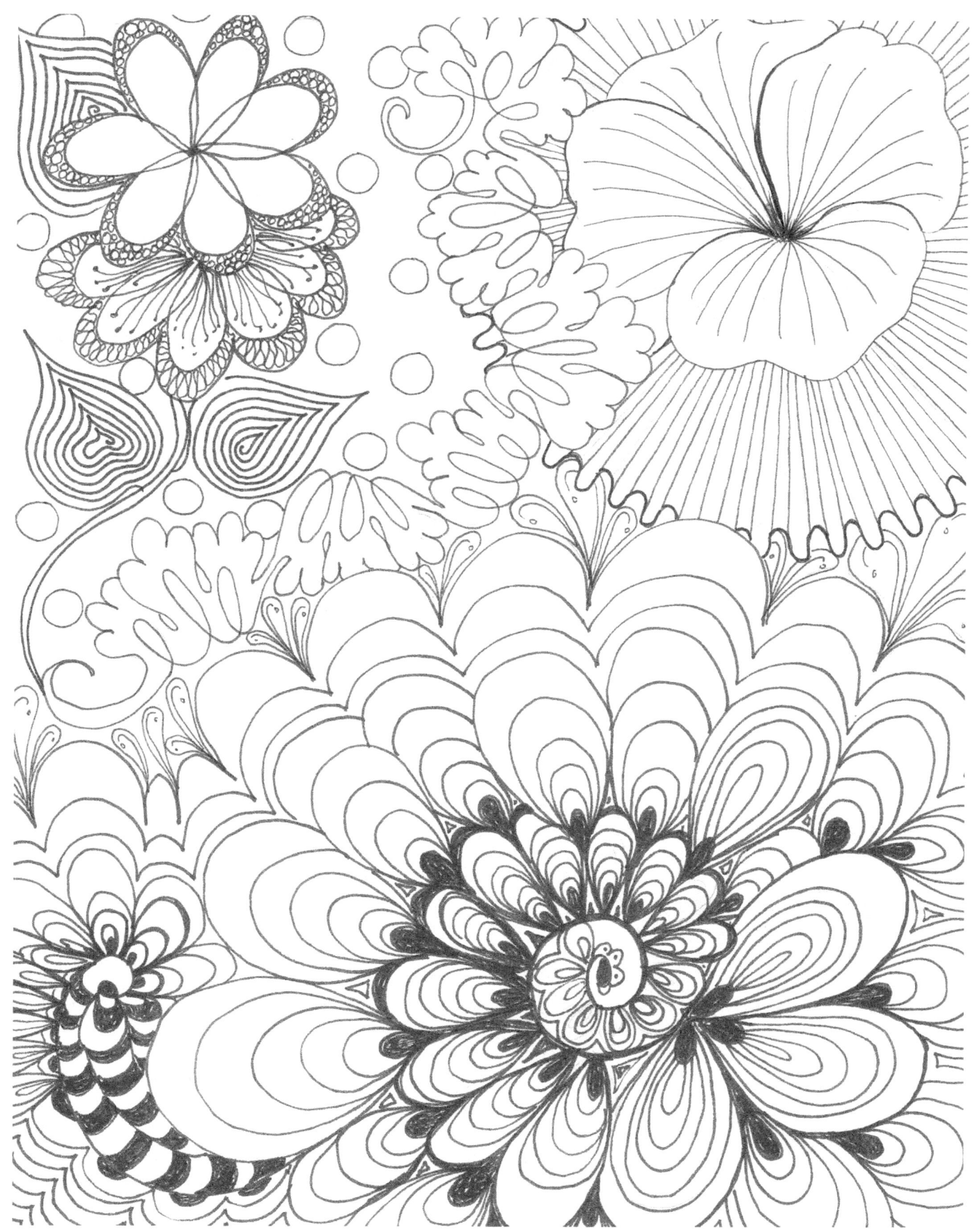

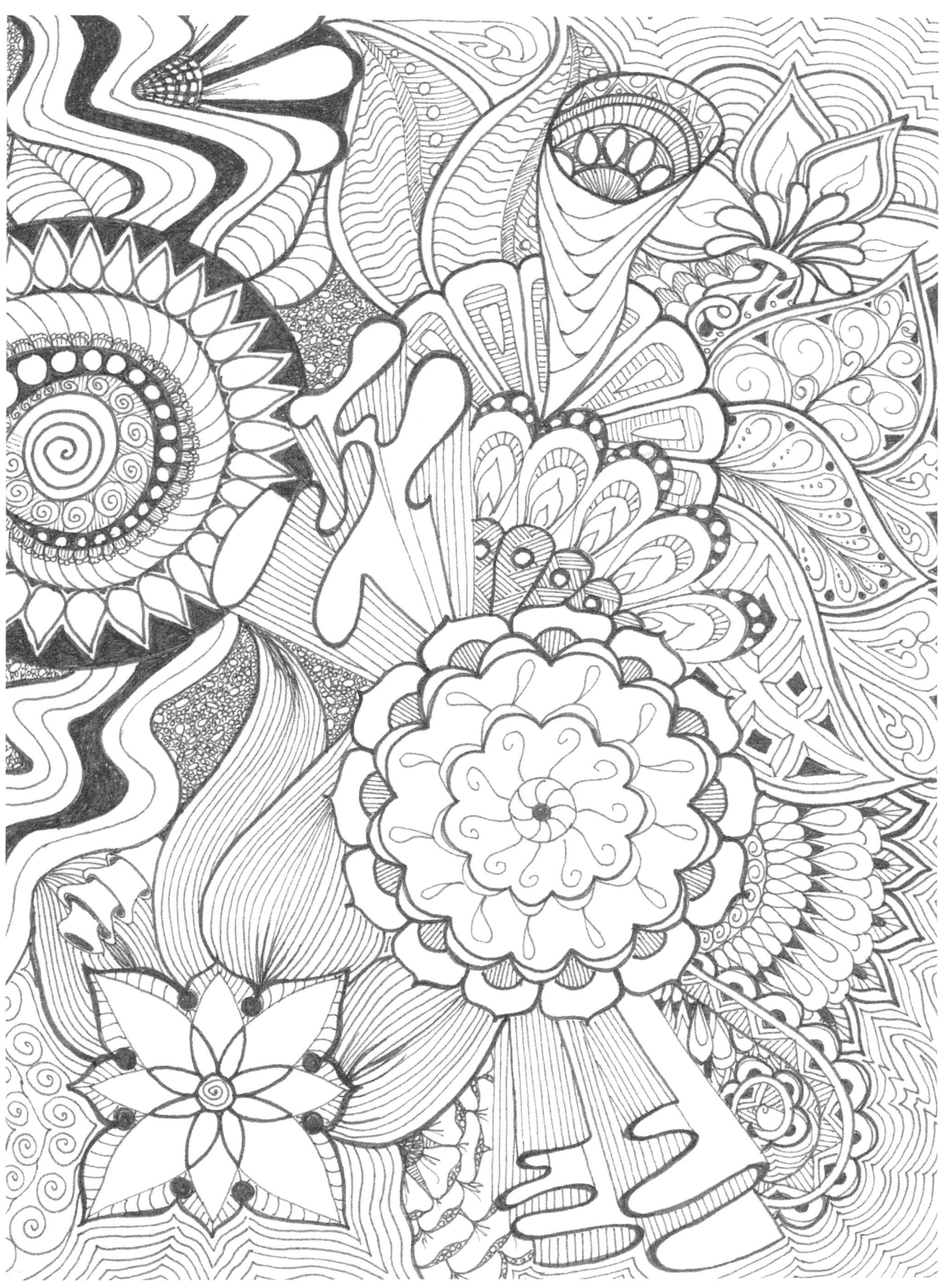

www.ingramcontent.com/pod-product-compliance
Lightning Source LLC
Chambersburg PA
CBHW080606190526
45169CB00007B/2906